Definitions of Woman

by

Alejandra Mora

This book is dedicated to the memory of my grandmother, the matriarch of our family.

We are lost without you,

but you remain alive in our hearts forever.

Introduction

To say women are strong is the understatement of this decade. We are surrounded and suffocated by the negativity, neglect and mistreatment by the powerful men in office telling us that our words don't count, our cries will not be heard, that our experiences with abuse don't matter. Women have been oppressed, abused, discarded, devalued, beaten and raped. We will take no more, especially during this supposed age of equality.

We will be heard in this world that wants nothing but to silence our voices, in the world that wants us to keep quiet about our opinions, our beliefs, our truths, a world that is slowly trying to push us back in time, where we were only seen and not heard. Our voices will become the time machine to propel us back into the 21st century.

Women should not be afraid to speak loudly when they're angry, hurt, to speak about the frustration that comes from continuously being treated like second class citizens. We need to be reminded to fight back with every gesture, every word and every action.

This book is not an attack on men. It's a reminder for women to not be stifled and not hide their beauty, intelligence, words and to remember that we can do anything that men can. The fact that we're compelled to do this is beyond me. We've gotten to a point where we've had to go back to grade school and be taught yet again that yes, we can play with that toy truck, drive the truck, or own the damn trucking company. We've had to talk to these grown men as if they were boys. "Be nice to the girls; don't touch them unless given permission, it's not funny to make fun of them or ridicule them, that words do hurt."

A reminder is necessary to whomever fails to see how far women have come, and that what's between a person's legs does not measure their worth. Together we will be heard and recognized.

I will begin with myself and then feel free to tell me who you are, your story, where your strength comes from.

I am a divorced single mom who struggles to find love, who has been hurt by men, beginning with the abandonment of my father when I was 3, the sexual harassment when I was 13 by a random man who'd go out of his way to make me uncomfortable on my way to school, the sexual assault by my first boyfriend when I was 17, verbal and emotional abuse in many subsequent relationships, not to mention being cheated on. These events have made me feel unworthy of love and affection, something everyone in this world should be entitled to.

Those experiences have had a tremendous impact on my life and have skewed my reality when it comes to the treatment I've allowed. I've at many times been confused about what's acceptable, what exactly is abuse and ultimately what is love.

After countless disappointments in relationships, hope seems like a faraway dream I'll just never attain. I am 39 years old, but I am still fighting, learning, and continuously working on being the best version of myself.

I am a single mother and we all know that is a job that is not easy; we question why we do it, yet in the same breath wouldn't have it any other way.

Being a sexual assault survivor as well has carried a heavy weight throughout my life, it was a trauma that changed me, impacting my choices and how I would carry myself. It added to the construction of the walls that I felt I had no choice but to build around me.

That's just my story. What's yours?

The life of a woman is never an easy one; we are faced with obstacles at every turn. But we do not let our experiences and trauma govern the path to our future. Recognizing our self-worth will be the guiding light, the reminder that we are not worthless.

Do not believe what you have been told with countless words and actions- that you don't matter, that you aren't good enough, not worth enough, that you do not deserve respect or love.

Do not let the voices of evil travel into your minds attempting to change who you really are. Don't let the obstacles define you; find yourself despite them.

Let this book serve as a reminder to anyone lost and afraid, that there is more you can do than sit in silence. Women can and will do and be anything.

This is for you, for us, for our daughters, our mothers, our friends.

(A message to those of us who are hiding and afraid, please join us in your hearts first until it is safe to speak loud and proud with us.)

Woman: Noun, Verb.

She...

does not beg anyone to be with her
knows her worth and does not
need anyone to validate it.

does not ignore red flags.

will not settle.

She will not…

put up with abuse,

surrender her power,

tolerate excuses,

change for anyone.

She will always:

put her children before everyone else,

see the beauty in all her imperfections,

love herself as she is.

She Demands Respect.

She Deserves Respect.

She…

does not let anyone's presence or
absence disrupt her goals,

has hope even when it all seems lost,

does for others out of the goodness of
her heart but knows when to stop if
she feels she's being used,

will not put up with liars, haters,
cheaters, abusers and overall assholes.

She:

forgives so that she can move on.

lets herself cry, dries her beautiful face,

takes a breath and begins again.

She will never: give her body to someone who does not deserve her heart.

She will never: stop believing in love

She will never: forget that the greatest love begins within herself.

She will never: let anyone's opinion of her affect how she sees herself

She will never: be silent when disrespected

She knows how to…

find comfort in silence and find peace in chaos.

take in the lessons and begin to heal.

be bigger person and knows and when to walk away.

be careful whom she gives her heart to but forgives herself if she chooses the wrong person

love her body the way it is and only makes changes if it is what she desires and not on the whim of a superficial man who doesn't deserve her anyway.

She will only lie beside someone

who is worthy of her:

time, presence, beauty, spirit, soul,

life, and love

- She does not let romantic relationships define her happiness
- She keeps away from toxic people
- She does not associate herself with anyone who wants to bring her down.
- She loves purely but with caution
- She protects her heart.

She speaks up when she is hurt-

and if she is not heard, is dismissed or misunderstood, she speaks up again, and this time, louder.

She does not let anyone stifle her brilliance.

We:

know when to ask for help.

wear colors in a drab world.

lift each other up, with support, love
and sisterhood.

rock high heels even if we're the tallest
woman in the room.

proudly show off our natural hair,
weave, perm, our beautiful bald head
with power and poise.

do not cater to anyone but ourselves
and our children.

She beats cancer.

She is a **survivor.**

On Sex:

She is the only one who decides
when, where, and if she is ready

She can sleep with whomever she
wants

She can abstain until marriage

She can want it today and not
tomorrow

She can have a headache

She can have a one-night stand

She can say No...

#MeToo

She knows sexual abuse, assault and
rape is not a result of what she's
wearing or because of anything she
has said

She knows she is not to blame

She can be sensual and not have that
misconstrued as an invitation to be
taken advantage of, or not given the
same respect all women deserve

It is **not** her fault and she will **never**
forget

28

In other words, on Rape:

NO means NO

A Word, from Me to You:

If you are sexually harassed, assaulted, or raped, tell someone, anyone that you can trust. You don't have to remain afraid and alone. If you want to, tell me, I will listen and help in any way that I can.

Now, you must know that your scarred reflection is only temporary. What you are seeing- is not the real woman that you are on the inside, nor is it the woman you will grow to become.

You will make it.

There is life after this moment.

It is ok to be afraid.

It is ok to cry, because I have cried.

It is normal to blame yourself because
I blamed myself.

You will survive because I am
surviving; we all are, every day.

You will heal.

Remember, that you are not alone.

Because, MeToo.

The time has come to wave your Pride
Flags!

Women can be:

gay

straight

bisexual

bicurious

gender fluid

demisexual

queer

transgendered

intersex

asexual

gender variant

pansexual

genderqueer

androgynous

Forgive me if I left anyone out; you

are all gorgeous-

so, shine on, stay proud and fuck the

haters.

On Love...

- Love is not an emotion of convenience or conditions

- It contains more beauty than the center of a star

- She knows that the right one won't come along until she lets the wrong ones go

- She will not allow herself to be taken for granted

- She can fall in love at any age

- She does not need anyone to validate her

- She can have faith in love and fall as many times as her heart can stand it

- She is always worthy

This Woman We Speak Of-

- She forgives herself

- She strives to live the life she's always dreamed of

- She can stick to her goals even if everyone around her thinks she won't make it

- She is not ashamed by how good she is in bed.

- She can have a one-night stand

- She can get divorced

- She can sleep with women

- She can find family in friends and enemies in family

- She can start over

She is a still a Woman if she…

has been sexually mutilated

does not have a uterus

has been raped

cannot bear children

does not want children

has had a mastectomy

is gay

is transgendered

On Being a Mother

She can raise her children however she
wants

She can take her children away from
an unsafe home

Her love is not conditional on her
child's sexual orientation

She raises her children to respect the
differences of others

She guides and leads and loves as best
as she can

She can give a child up for adoption

and does not have to explain her

reasons to anyone

and

She **can** have an abortion-

and it is her **choice** to wait until she is

ready to become a mother

The List goes on…

- She can hear advice and still choose to follow her own way

- She can choose to spend her time with anyone she wants

- She can be alone

- She can go back to an ex if she wants to forgive

- She doesn't feel the need to explain herself to anyone

- She lives by her own rules

- She answers to only herself and her God

- She can be a believer in a world of atheists

- She can be outspoken in a land that is used to women who are silenced

- She can fight for her country

- She can fight for what she believes in

- She can vote for whomever she wants

- She can choose to not vote at all if she supports no one

- She can protest, and her voice will not be lost in the crowd

- She proudly speaks the language of her homeland in a country that locks her children in cages

- She admits when she has a problem

- She is not ashamed if she needs therapy

- She knows when someone does not deserve her love

- She recognizes that she is the prize- and not a consolation prize

- She knows the difference between promises and follow-through

- She focuses on herself when she needs to

- She knows that love grows over time

- She knows she has the right to demand the love and respect she's worthy of

- She does not rush something that can last forever

- She cannot be held down, for she has wings

- She is in love with the color of her skin, the shape of her body, the content of her character

- She can pray: to her God, a statue, the universe, the angels, her ancestors or not at all

- She knows to be the treasure and not the seeker

- She knows when to step back and look at the bigger picture

- She breathes through pain and does not dwell on what she cannot change

- She admits when she is wrong

- She discards anyone who does not deserve her

- She knows when it is time to move on
- She knows it's ok to make mistakes
- She wears her strength like a suit of armor
- She surrounds herself with positivity
- She learns from others
- She knows tomorrow is a new day
- She can miss someone who hurt her-but finds the strength in her self-worth to stay away

- She gives herself a break

- She is compassionate

- She is aware plans can change

- She doesn't let anyone change how she views herself

- She knows relationships are not all romance and perfection but hard work and sacrifice

- If someone wants to leave her, she lets them go because she knows she is worth fighting for

- She defends herself, her home,
  her family, her heart

- She believes in what you do,
  not what you say

- She can call bullshit from a mile
  away

- She creates the future she wants
  for herself

- She knows when to let go

- She does not wait for anyone to
  dictate how her life will go
  because she's already on the
  path to her future and never
  looks back.

- She embraces her flaws
- She doesn't let anyone take away her smile
- A failed relationship will not derail the plans for her life
- She lifts her spirit knowing true happiness lies within
- She goes after what she wants
- She knows how to laugh at herself

- She dances like no one is watching-when in fact everyone is

- She treats others how she would want to be treated

- She pursues her education at any age

- She knows when to walk away

- She is not afraid to walk away from what causes her pain

- She knows that sometimes goodbye is all that's left to say

- She faces each day tougher than the one before

Last Word

She holds a heart in her chest that can care for the world, yet it is also an impenetrable shield, because she's a woman of this world, where people are far from perfect, where sadly she has learned there are many that are out to harm her, stifle her, silence her. She is aware of those who strive to keep her from rising above the flames of this war. She has been forced to become protective of herself, wary of the dangers she faces, and she is ready to fight back.

She is a fighting survivor, a champion of life and love, an example for all of who struggle, who live out of fear, who are on the way to success and self-love but haven't quite gotten there yet. She is our guide, she is the goal. She can do it all.

She is the Definition of Woman.

<u>Woman. Mother. Daughter. Sister. Friend.</u>
<u>She. Her. Me. Us.</u>

She is free to do and be

anything she wants.

With the standards set by her own

rules,

She will live her greatest, fullest

and proudest life.

Her voice will be heard,

Because it is the loudest of them

all.

About the Author

Alejandra Mora is a poet and author from New York City, where she currently resides with her 16-year-old daughter.

Books:

Memories of Fog

Definitions of Woman

Instagram @poemsbyalejandra

Twitter @alejandra_poems

Facebook: PoetAlejandraMora

Thank you for reading.

www.ingramcontent.com/pod-product-compliance
Lightning Source LLC
LaVergne TN
LVHW020102190726
843498LV00014B/2145